Safe to Speak:

A Survivor's Guide to Navigating Conflict Without Fear

Lisa Nicole Thiombiano M.S.

Lisa Nicole Publishing
Orlando, FL 32824
www.healanddevelop.com

ISBN: 978-1-968085-01-8
Printed in the United States of America

Introduction
Conflict Isn't the Enemy

For many of us who have survived abuse, the word *conflict* carries a heavy weight. It sounds like yelling. Like fear. Like silence after slammed doors and bruised hearts. It sounds like danger, and our nervous systems remember.

After abuse, conflict often feels like something to be avoided at all costs. We stay silent. We shrink. We become experts at reading the room, preemptively apologizing, or walking on eggshells. We do anything to avoid what once led to pain.

But here's the truth that healing gently reveals:
Not all conflict is unsafe.
Some conflict is healthy. Some conflict is necessary. And in the right hands, conflict can be *good.* It can be the place where truth is spoken, needs are named, and growth begins.

Conflict isn't the enemy. **Abuse is.**
Control, manipulation, disrespect, and fear- that's what made conflict feel dangerous before. But *speaking up* for yourself is not dangerous. Saying "I need," "I feel," or even "I disagree" isn't harmful, it's human and its necessary.
Healing means learning to tell the difference.

This guide is not just about tolerating conflict. It's about *reclaiming your voice.*

It's about grounding your body, setting new boundaries, and walking through disagreement without reliving the trauma of your past. It's about learning how to *stay* in the room. Be calm, clear, and centered, without abandoning yourself or attacking others.

Whether you're learning to have difficult conversations in your marriage, parenting through tough moments, managing conflict in the workplace, or simply learning to say no, this guide will walk with you, step by step.

With each chapter, you'll not only gain knowledge, but practical tools you can use today. You'll learn how to protect your peace *without losing your power.*

If you've ever thought:

- "I shut down in every argument."

- "I'm scared of what I might say or do when I get angry."

- "I'd rather say nothing than start a fight."

- "When someone raises their voice, I freeze."

Then this book is for you. You are not broken. You are healing and you are learning. And your voice whether shaky, strong, or somewhere in between, is *worth hearing.*

Chapter 1

Understanding Your Conflict Blueprint

"Before we change how we respond to conflict, we have to understand why we respond the way we do."

Everyone has a *conflict blueprint.* It is an emotional map shaped by experience. Before you ever spoke up for yourself, you were taught (directly or indirectly) what conflict looks, sounds, and feels like.

If you grew up in a home where yelling meant danger, or where silence was used as punishment, your body may now interpret *any* tension as threat.

If you were in an abusive relationship where disagreement led to punishment, manipulation, or isolation, you may still freeze, fawn, or flee at the first sign of friction.

That blueprint isn't a flaw. It's a survival strategy.

But healing means reworking the blueprint. It is not erasing what you've been through, but building something safer and stronger on top of it.

Your Conflict Style: Fight, Flight, Freeze, or Fawn

These responses aren't just theoretical, they're embodied trauma patterns. Let's break them down:

- **Fight:** You meet conflict with intensity, anger, arguing, or defensiveness. You may speak loudly, interrupt, or try to *win* the disagreement.

- **Flight:** You avoid conflict at all costs. You might leave the room, change the subject, or ghost the person entirely.

- **Freeze:** Your body shuts down. You go numb, mentally check out, or feel paralyzed and unable to respond.

- **Fawn:** You try to make everything okay. You people-please, apologize unnecessarily, or take responsibility for things that aren't yours.

You might recognize yourself in more than one style depending on the situation or person and that's okay.

Practice Step 1: Identify Your Default Conflict Style

Reflection Prompt:

Think back to the last 2–3 disagreements you had. What did your body do? What were your first thoughts?

Were you angry? Anxious? Silent? Did you try to smooth it over or walk away?

Journaling Exercise:

Write down your most common responses under pressure. What does your voice do? Your body? Your mind?

Example: "When someone raises their voice at me, I immediately shut down and can't form words. My chest tightens and I just want to get out of the room."

_____

_____

_____

_____

_____

_____

_____

_____

_____

Practice Step 2: Trace the Blueprint

Where did you learn your current style?

Think about:

- How conflict was handled in your family growing up

- What you witnessed in past relationships

- How safe you felt expressing disagreement as a child or partner

Prompt:

"In my childhood, conflict looked like…"

"In past relationships, speaking up meant…"

"Now, when I try to express my needs, I feel…"

This helps connect past trauma to present patterns, not to blame—but to understand.

Awareness gives you power.

_____

_____

_____

_____

_____

_____

Practice Step 3: What Do You *Want* Your Style to Be?

Healing doesn't mean becoming fearless, it means becoming *anchored*.

What would it feel like to approach conflict with:

- Calm?

- Clarity?

- Respect for yourself *and* others?

Write a vision of your "healed" conflict style.

"When I feel upset, I breathe before responding. I speak directly but gently. I stay in the conversation, even when it's uncomfortable. I trust I can be safe *and* honest."

_____

_____

_____

_____

_____

_____

_____

_____

_____

Tool: Your Conflict Style Map

See below the four columns labeled:

- **Fight**
- **Flight**
- **Freeze**
- **Fawn**

Under each one, list moments from your past when that was your default.

Then circle which one shows up the most *today.*

Finally, write what new pattern you'd like to practice in those moments.

Fight	Flight	Freeze	Fawn

Chapter 2:

Safety First. Grounding Yourself During Disagreement

> **"You are allowed to pause. You are allowed to breathe. You are allowed to feel safe, even in hard conversations."**

For survivors of abuse, conflict can feel like danger because the body remembers. Your heart races. Your palms sweat. Your voice disappears. Your nervous system isn't overreacting, it's doing exactly what it was trained to do: *protect you from harm.*

But here's the truth:
You're not in danger anymore.
You're just having a disagreement.
And your body may need help remembering that.

Before we dive into communication techniques or conflict resolution strategies, we have to address the one thing that makes everything else possible: **your sense of internal safety**.

When you feel grounded in your body, you can choose your response instead of reacting out of fear.

What Safety Looks Like in Conflict:

- You can breathe fully.

- You know you can pause without punishment.

- You trust your voice won't betray you.

- You feel connected to your body, not outside of it.

Practice Step 1: Know Your Triggers

Objective: Recognize the early warning signs of escalation so you can ground before reacting.

Prompt:
Think of a time conflict became overwhelming. What triggered you?

Was it…

- A raised voice?
- A certain phrase?
- Being interrupted?
- Someone walking toward you quickly?

Journal Exercise:

List your common *conflict triggers*. Then beside each one, write:

- What that trigger reminds you of

- How your body usually responds

Example: *"When someone says, 'You're too sensitive,' I shut down because it reminds me of my abuser mocking me."*

Awareness = power. When you name the trigger, you take the first step toward controlling your response.

_____

_____

_____

_____

_____

_____

Practice Step 2: Use the 3x3x3 Grounding Method

This simple but powerful technique brings your body out of fight-or-flight in less than a minute.

The 3x3x3 Method:

1. **Name 3 things you can see**

2. **Touch 3 things and describe their texture**

3. **Say 3 affirmations out loud**

   Examples: "I am safe." "I can stay present." "This is not the past."

Use this before, during, or after a hard conversation. It's your nervous system's reset button.

Practice Step 3: Create a Personal Safety Plan for Conflict

This is your personal rescue map for what to do when conflict gets overwhelming.

Your Safety Plan Might Include:

- A phrase you can say to pause: *"I need a moment to gather my thoughts."*

- A grounding tool: Holding a textured item like a stone, bracelet, or cloth

- A body anchor: Pressing your feet into the floor or placing your hand on your chest

- A post-conflict routine: Journaling, prayer, music, or a trusted person to debrief with

Worksheet Prompt:

"When I feel overwhelmed, I will…"

"Before a hard conversation, I will…"

"If I get triggered, I will…"

_____

_____

_____

_____

_____

_____

_____

_____

_____

Tool: Conflict Grounding Checklist

Print this and keep it somewhere visible.

- Have I eaten or hydrated today?

- Am I in a private, safe space for this conversation?

- Can I feel my feet on the ground?

- Have I done a few deep breaths before beginning?

- Do I have permission to pause if needed?

You are not weak for needing support. You are wise for preparing.

Chapter 3:

Boundaries in Conflict

> "Boundaries are not walls, they are doors with locks. They don't shut people out. They teach people how to come in."

One of the most common fears for survivors is this:
If I speak up, will I lose the relationship?

But here's a truth that transforms everything:
Boundaries don't break relationship, broken boundaries do.

When you've lived through abuse, your boundaries were often ignored, mocked, or punished. Over time, you may have learned that it's safer to stay silent than to speak your truth. But healing requires you to draw new lines. Lines that protect your peace without punishing others.

In this chapter, you'll learn how to hold boundaries *during* conflict, not just after it. Because real healing isn't just about saying *no*, it's about staying present while protecting yourself.

What Boundaries in Conflict Look Like:

- Saying "I'm not ready to talk about that right now."

- Asking for space instead of storming out

- Naming what is or isn't okay without accusation

- Knowing when to pause, not disappear

Boundaries are your bridge back to yourself.

Practice Step 1: Understand the Purpose of Boundaries

Prompt: What do you believe about boundaries?

Circle any thoughts that resonate:

- "They'll just make things worse."

- "People will leave me if I set them."

- "I'm being selfish if I say no."

- "I don't want to hurt anyone."

Now reframe:

Boundaries don't push people away. They protect what matters most: *your voice, your values, and your emotional safety.*

Practice Step 2: Use Boundary Scripts During Conflict

Here are trauma-informed ways to set clear, non-aggressive boundaries in real time:

- "I want to talk about this, but I need to do it calmly. Let's take a break."

- "I'm willing to continue if we both agree to speak respectfully."

- "I'm not okay with being interrupted. Can I finish my thought?"

- "I don't feel safe right now. I need some time before we continue."

Your Turn:

Fill in the blanks to create your own go-to responses, then create some below:

- "I need _____ before I can continue."

- "It's not okay with me when _____."

- "In order for me to feel safe, I need _____."

_____

_____

_____

_____

_____

_____

_____

_____

_____

_____

Practice Step 3: Learn How to Pause Without Abandoning

Walking away in silence or slamming a door feels powerful, but it's not the same as a *healthy pause*.

How to Pause the Right Way:

- Clearly state that you're pausing, not leaving for good
    "I need 20 minutes to gather myself. Let's come back to this."

- Avoid ghosting. Use boundaries, not avoidance.

- Offer to return when you're ready—this builds trust and safety.

Worksheet Prompt:

"When I'm overwhelmed, I will say _____."

"To signal a pause without shutting down, I'll use _____

(gesture, phrase, plan)."

_____

_____

_____

_____

_____

_____

_____

_____

_____

_____

Tool: Conflict Boundary Builder

Draw three columns:

- **What triggers me**
- **What I need in that moment**
- **How I can express it kindly**

Example:

- Trigger: Being talked over
- Need: To be heard fully
- Kind Boundary: "Please let me finish. I'll give you the same respect."

What triggers me	What I need in that moment	How I can express it kindly

Chapter 4

How to Disagree Without Destroying Connection

> "A disagreement doesn't mean disconnection. It means two people are showing up with truth."

One of the greatest lies abuse teaches us is this:

If someone is upset with you, love is leaving.

So we either silence ourselves to keep the peace… or we erupt in fear when conflict surfaces. Because to us, conflict has always meant danger or abandonment.

But here's the truth: Healthy people disagree.

Safe relationships survive tension.

Disagreement can actually deepen intimacy, *when it's done well.*

The goal of conflict isn't to win. It's to understand. And when two people can disagree with curiosity, respect, and presence, they build something sacred: *trust.*

What Healthy Disagreement Sounds Like:

- "I hear what you're saying. Can I share my view?"

- "I disagree, but I'm still listening."

- "We see this differently, and that's okay."

- "Let's figure this out together."

Practice Step 1: Use the Feel–Need–Request Formula

When emotions are high, communication gets messy. Use this three-part sentence to stay clear, calm, and kind:

"I feel ___ because I need ___. Can we ___?"

Examples:

- "I feel overwhelmed because I need more time to think. Can we take a break and talk again later?"

- "I feel dismissed because I need to be heard. Can we both take turns sharing?"

Your Turn:

Fill in 3 examples from recent or imagined conflict:

1. I feel _____ because I need _____. Can we _____?

2. I feel _____ because I need _____. Can we _____?

3. I feel _____ because I need _____ . Can we
   _____ ?

This structure helps you stay present and speak from the heart—without attacking.

Practice Step 2: Try Reflective Listening

In every argument, the biggest thing people want is to feel heard. Reflective listening creates connection even when you disagree.

How to do it:

1. Listen fully (without interrupting).
2. Repeat back what you heard, using your own words.
3. Ask: "Did I get that right?"
4. Then share your perspective.

"So, what I'm hearing is that you felt hurt when I canceled. That it made you feel like a low priority. Is that right?"

This doesn't mean you agree. It means you're listening with respect. And that builds safety.

Practice Exercise:
Role-play in your journal or with a partner. Take a common disagreement and walk through both sides using this format.

Practice Step 3: Use the Conflict Repair Checklist

When a conversation gets heated, you need a way back to peace. Use this checklist to reset:

- Did I speak with honesty *and* kindness?
- Did I listen without preparing my comeback?
- Did I take a break if I got overwhelmed?
- Did I name my needs without blame?
- Did we leave the conversation with clarity?

If not, go back. Repair isn't weakness. It's wisdom.

Tool: The "Pause, Paraphrase, Proceed" Method

Use this in real-time conflict to stay grounded:

- **Pause:** Take a breath before responding.
- **Paraphrase:** Repeat what you heard to show understanding.
- **Proceed:** Share your response using the Feel–Need–Request method.

It might feel mechanical at first, but it trains your nervous system to *stay* present instead of shutting down or spiraling.

Chapter 5

Conflict in Relationships You Want to Keep

> **"If it matters to you, conflict will find its way there. But so can love, repair, and growth."**

Some relationships are easy to walk away from when conflict arises, coworkers, acquaintances, even certain family members. But what happens when the person you're clashing with is someone you love? Your spouse. Your child. A close friend. A trusted leader. Someone you want to stay connected to.

That's when conflict feels the most confusing.
Because suddenly you're not just protecting your peace, you're trying to protect the relationship, too.
And for survivors, that often leads to a painful question:
Can I speak up... and still be loved?

The answer is *yes*.
But it requires skills you may never have been taught: healthy repair, respectful disagreement, and boundaries that make room for closeness.

This chapter walks you through what to do when the relationship matters, and the conversation gets hard.

What Healthy Conflict Looks Like in Close Relationships

- You're not afraid of "messy moments" because you know repair is possible.

- You disagree, but you don't withdraw love.

- You give and receive feedback without blame or fear.

- You both own your part and protect the connection.

Practice Step 1: Identify Safe vs. Unsafe Relationships for Growth

Not every relationship is ready for conflict growth.

Safe relationships allow you to be imperfect and honest without retaliation.

Unsafe ones punish, manipulate, or dismiss you when you express yourself.

Ask:

- Does this person listen when I speak?

- Do I feel calmer or more anxious after we argue?

- Do they take responsibility or always shift the blame?

- Can we disagree and still feel close?

Journal Prompt:

"The relationships in my life where I feel safest to be honest are…"

"The ones where I shrink the most are…"

This helps you know where to invest—and where to tread gently.

_____

_____

_____

_____

_____

_____

_____

_____

_____

_____

Practice Step 2: Use the Circle of Repair

When conflict happens in meaningful relationships, the goal isn't to win, it's to reconnect.

The Circle of Repair

1. **Pause** – Take time to regulate your nervous system
2. **Reflect** – Own your part, without shame or over-responsibility
3. **Reach Out** – With softness and intention (not pressure)
4. **Reconnect** – Share impact, ask for what you need, and invite theirs
5. **Reset** – Agree on new boundaries or next steps

Example:

"Earlier, I got defensive and cut you off. That wasn't okay. I care about what you were saying. Can we try again?"

Practice Step 3: Write a Repair Letter

Some conversations are best started on paper, especially when emotions are still high.

Use this format to write a letter to someone you love:

"When [this happened], I felt _____.

I recognize I may have _____.

I want to understand your experience and share mine.

I care about this relationship and want to find a way forward."

Even if you don't send the letter, writing it helps you clarify your heart and create space for healing.

Tool: Healthy Conflict Agreements

Sit down with someone you love and create a shared agreement about how you'll handle hard conversations.

Examples:

- "We'll take turns speaking without interrupting."

- "If one of us gets overwhelmed, we'll take a 20-minute break."

- "We will not yell, curse, or insult during conflict."

- "After conflict, we'll check in the next day with kindness."

This becomes your emotional safety net. A shared plan for when things get tough.

Chapter 6

The Art of Assertiveness

> **"I am not too much. I am not too quiet. I am not wrong for needing what I need."**

After surviving abuse, many of us swing between two extremes:

- We either *stay silent* and let things slide…
- Or we *explode* after staying quiet too long.

Neither one feels good. Neither one brings peace.

But there is a third way.

It's not silence.

It's not shouting.

It's **assertiveness**. The calm, grounded middle ground where your voice has both clarity and kindness.

Assertiveness says: *"I matter, and so do you."*

It honors your needs without steamrolling anyone else's. And the more you practice it, the safer your world becomes.

What Assertiveness Looks and Sounds Like

- You speak clearly, without apologizing for your truth.

- You hold boundaries *and* compassion.

- You ask for what you need without guilt or shame.

- You don't raise your voice, you raise your value.

Practice Step 1: Know the Difference Between Passive, Aggressive, and Assertive

Passive

- "It's fine." (When it's not.)

- "I don't want to cause trouble."

- You shrink, avoid, or people-please.

Aggressive

- "You always do this!"

- "You don't care how I feel."

- You attack, raise your voice, or shut others down.

Assertive

- "I felt hurt when that happened. Can we talk about it?"

- "I need some space right now. Let's revisit this later."

- You express yourself clearly and calmly, with respect for both parties.

Reflection Prompt:

"When I speak up, I tend to lean more toward _____ (passive / aggressive / assertive)."

"What stops me from being more assertive is _____."

Practice Step 2: Use the "I Statement" Formula

This simple tool helps you speak with ownership, not blame.

"I feel ___ when ___. I need ___."

Examples:

- "I feel overwhelmed when I'm interrupted. I need a chance to finish my thoughts."

- "I feel anxious when our plans change without notice. I need us to check in beforehand."

Now try your own:

1. I feel _____ when _____ . I need _____ .

2. I feel _____ when _____ . I need _____ .

3. I feel _____ when _____ . I need _____ .

The goal isn't to control the other person—it's to *communicate clearly* and protect your peace.

_____

_____

_____

_____

_____

_____

_____

_____

_____

_____

Practice Step 3: Practice Assertiveness in Safe, Low-Risk Situations

Don't wait until you're emotionally charged to start.

Begin by practicing assertiveness in small, safe places:

- Asking for your drink order to be corrected

- Saying "no" to extra work or responsibilities

- Telling a friend you need quiet time

- Asking for help, instead of doing it all alone

Challenge Prompt:

This week, I will practice assertiveness by _____.

If I feel fear, I will remind myself _____.

Tool: Assertive Communication Cheat Sheet

Keep these phrases in your back pocket when you need them:

- "That doesn't work for me."

- "I'm not comfortable with that."

- "Let me get back to you on that."

- "I want to talk about this, but I need to do it calmly."

- "I respect your opinion. I see things differently."

Repeat them aloud. Practice them in the mirror.

Make them your own.

Chapter 7

When Conflict Feels Unsafe — Red Flags to Watch For

> "If your voice costs you your safety, it's not a conversation, it's a warning."

Not all conflict is healthy.

Not every disagreement is a growth opportunity.

Some conflict is actually **control in disguise**.

For survivors, one of the hardest things to do is trust yourself enough to walk away. Not because you're giving up, but because you finally understand: *Not every conflict deserves your energy.*

There is a difference between a healthy disagreement that can lead to healing, and a toxic exchange that chips away at your sense of worth. You are not here to fix abuse with maturity. You are not responsible for making dysfunction digestible.

In this chapter, you'll learn how to **spot unsafe conflict, set protective limits**, and **give yourself permission to exit the cycle of harm.**

Signs You're in an Unsafe Conflict Pattern

- You're constantly walking on eggshells, afraid to "set them off."

- You feel confused or guilty after every disagreement.

- You're punished (emotionally or physically) for setting boundaries.

- The other person gaslights, mocks, or invalidates your feelings.

- You never feel heard, only controlled, manipulated, or silenced.

Practice Step 1: Learn the 3 D's of Toxic Conflict

Watch for patterns, not just one-time mistakes. If any of these are present *frequently*, the conflict is likely unsafe:

1. Disrespect

- Yelling, cursing, name-calling

- Eye-rolling, mocking, dismissiveness

- Talking *at* you instead of *with* you

2. Deflection

- Blame-shifting: "You're too sensitive."

- Never taking responsibility

- Changing the subject when you try to address an issue

3. Domination

- Trying to "win" instead of understand
- Using guilt, shame, or threats to control the outcome
- Withholding affection or connection when you speak your truth

Reflection Prompt:

"Which of these behaviors have I normalized in the name of love?"

"Which ones show up in my current or past relationships?"

Practice Step 2: Set a Safety Boundary

In unsafe conflict, *leaving the room* is not disrespectful, it's essential.

You are allowed to say:

- "I'm not staying in this conversation if it turns disrespectful."
- "I will not be spoken to like this. I'm leaving now, and we can talk later if it's safe."
- "This feels emotionally unsafe for me. I'm protecting my peace."

Journal Prompt:

"When conflict crosses into danger for me, I will _____."

"I give myself permission to _____ without guilt or explanation."

_____

_____

_____

_____

_____

_____

_____

_____

_____

_____

Practice Step 3: Listen to Your Body, Not Just Their Words

Sometimes, unsafe conflict doesn't look loud, it feels *tight*.
Tense. Suffocating. Quietly punishing.
You know it in your chest, your gut, your throat. Start paying attention to your *body's cues.*

Body Red Flags:

- Shallow breathing

- Nausea or clenched stomach

- Shaking hands or legs

- Feeling mentally foggy or frozen

- Going numb or dissociating

Tool:

Begin tracking your physical responses during difficult conversations. What do you feel? What shifts? When do you *start* to feel unsafe? Your body is not betraying you.
It's protecting you.

Tool: "Is This Conversation Safe?" Self-Check

Before or during a difficult conversation, ask:

- Am I being respected?

- Is my voice being heard without retaliation?

- Can I leave the conversation if I feel unsafe?

- Is this a disagreement… or a power struggle?

If the answer to any of these is no—pause. Protect. Exit if needed.

Chapter 8

Rewriting the Narrative. Conflict as a Tool for Growth

> "Every time I use my voice with love and truth, I rebuild the world inside me."

You've made it through the fire, facing fears, setting boundaries, learning your body, listening to your truth.

Now comes the most transformative step of all: **reframing conflict not as something to fear... but something that can *grow you.***

When you've lived through emotional harm, conflict feels like something to survive. But in healing, conflict becomes something you can *engage with, safely, fully, and freely.*

You can disagree without shutting down. You can assert your truth without guilt. You can hold hard conversations with your head high and your heart open.

This chapter is about *rewriting the story.*

From "Conflict means I'm not safe,"

to: **"Conflict can mean I'm ready to be seen."**

What Reframed Conflict Feels Like

- You feel *tension* in your body—but not terror

- You stay in the conversation long enough to reach truth

- You know how to pause, repair, and protect

- You leave the moment wiser, not wounded

Practice Step 1: Reframe What Conflict Means to You

Old beliefs survivors often hold:

- "Conflict means I'll be punished or abandoned."

- "If someone's mad at me, I did something wrong."

- "If I speak up, I'll ruin the relationship."

Let's replace those with healing truths:

New narratives to choose from:

- "Conflict is not the absence of love, it's a test of it."

- "I can be imperfect and still worthy of respect."

- "If someone leaves because I'm honest, they weren't safe to begin with."

Reflection Prompt:

"One belief I want to release about conflict is…"

"One truth I want to carry forward is…"

Practice Step 2: Reflect on How Far You've Come

Look back at your earliest conflict patterns, then look at you now.

Prompt:

- "Then, I used to _____ when conflict came."
- "Now, I'm learning to _____."
- "I'm proud of how I handled _____."
- "I trust myself more because _____."

Celebrate yourself. Growth is loud *and* quiet.

Sometimes the real victory is staying present when you used to run.

Practice Step 3: Practice "Brave Disagreements" with Safe People

It's time to use what you've learned—*not perfectly,* but *bravely.*

Choose 1–2 safe, respectful people in your life and prepare to engage in a conversation where you:

- Share a boundary
- Express a disagreement
- Ask for a need to be met
- Reflect and repair if things get tense

Debrief Journal Prompt:

"What did I feel before, during, and after?"

"What went better than I expected?"

"What do I want to do differently next time?"

You are building muscle memory for peace.

_____

_____

_____

_____

_____

_____

_____

_____

Tool: Conflict Growth Journal Page

Use this after every disagreement to build emotional awareness and healing habits.

After the conversation, ask yourself:

- What did I do well?
- Where did I get triggered?
- What helped me stay grounded?
- What did I learn about myself?
- How did I honor both truth and tenderness?

The goal isn't perfection. It's progress rooted in self-respect.

_____

_____

_____

_____

_____

_____

_____

www.ingramcontent.com/pod-product-compliance
Lightning Source LLC
Chambersburg PA
CBHW072036060426
42449CB00010BA/2291